BIRDS
of
NORTH AMERICA

PHOTOGRAPHY AND TEXT BY

JIM ROETZEL

TWIN LIGHTS PUBLISHERS, ROCKPORT MASSACHUSETTS

First published in the United States of America by:

Twin Lights Publishers, Inc.
8 Hale Street
Rockport, Massachusetts 01966
Telephone: (978) 546-7398
http://www.twinlightspub.com

ISBN: 1-885435-80-0
ISBN: 978-1-885435-80-4

10 9 8 7 6 5 4 3 2 1

ATLANTIC PUFFIN COLONY (*opposite*)
Newfoundland, Canada

Like many auks, the Atlantic Puffin is counter
shaded. Against the bright ocean surface, its white
stomach camouflages it from predators below, and
its black back blends with the surface from above.

(*jacket front*)

Burrowing Owl, Cape Coral, Florida

(*jacket back, clockwise from top*)

Sandhill Cranes, Bosque del Apache, New Mexico
Northern Flicker, Noble County, Ohio
White-breasted Nuthatch, Cuyahoga Valley
National Park, Ohio

(*frontispiece*)

Indigo Bunting

Editor:
Sue Fuhs Barraclough

Book design by:
SYP Design & Production, Inc.
www.sypdesign.com

Printed in China

INTRODUCTION

When I started in nature photography in the early 1980s things were very different. Cameras were film-based, the choices of tripods and accessories were typically limited to local store inventory, and there were only a few hundred other photographers chasing birds. If you're familiar with photography, you'll find that the equipment I used to create the images in this book reflects the recent evolution of the field. The oldest photograph was taken with a Nikon F3 camera and 600mm/F5.6 manual Nikkor lens on Kodachrome film, many others were shot with a Canon EOS-3 camera and 600mm/F4 lens on Fuji Velvia, and the most recent photographs were captured using image stabilized lenses and digital single lens reflex cameras. The photographic tools have changed.

When contacted about this project by my publisher, I was very flattered and more than a little nervous. I have a great respect for the experts in the fields of ornithology and photography and I wanted this book to appeal to them as well as the novice or casual bird watcher. I was also surprised to realize that there were few books available with images that simply focus on communicating the joy of birds.

The burgeoning popularity of birding, the growth of the Internet, and the development of digital cameras has created an incredible swell of interest in bird photography. But the most essential tools have remained the same: a deep interest and understanding of natural history; a genuine love of wildlife; and a level of commitment that might appear to others to border on obsession. Most important, however, is the fact that in the end, it is all about the birds —their beauty, diversity, and inspiration.

Throughout the book, I have identified the location of each image. Photographs that were taken under controlled conditions are marked with a "CC" after their location. We have kept narrative to a minimum intentionally; there are numerous eloquent resources already available for identification.

Many of the images were taken in my home state of Ohio, especially in and around Cuyahoga Valley National Park. There are certain bird species that are most easily found in particular areas of the country and I have been fortunate to photograph Snow Geese in Bosque del Apache, Roseate Spoonbills in the Florida Everglades, Smith's Longspurs in the Alaskan Arctic, and Acorn Woodpeckers in the Madera Canyon of Arizona. Some of the photographs were simply taken "along the way" when all the elements—a cooperative bird in good plumage, in perfect light, set against the right background—lined up and I was fortunate enough to have my camera to capture the fleeting moment. Nothing compares to the magic and thrill when it all comes together.

Of course, for every great image there were dozens of missed opportunities. This is an inevitable part of bird photography. Yet, the memories of birds seen but not photographed are still vivid. Most young birds imprint instinctively on avian adults, food, and patterns and likewise, birds often make lasting impressions on birders and photographers. On many mornings, a bird's vibrant colors, song, or displays of affection have left their permanent mark on me.

Time in the field has taught me a few lessons about the art of bird photography, which have influenced my work. The first is the golden rule: *respect your subject*—the birds and the protection of their habitat are more important than your efforts to get the photograph. While the iconic birds are easy to make look good, it's important to represent the flitting songbirds in your backyard with equal beauty. The best photographers recognize and capture the same dignity in a chickadee as they do in an eagle.

You must also dedicate yourself to learning as much as you can about birds. You have to study their habitats, food sources, behaviors, calls, and idiosyncrasies. The more you know about their natural history, the better a photographer you will become. You'll be able to anticipate a photo opportunity that truly reflects a bird's character and spirit. While it is certainly important to learn the technical tools of photography, remember that cameras, lenses, and tripods are just objects—they don't take photographs by themselves. Compared to your understanding and passion for birds, camera knowledge is secondary.

Finally, I have learned that of all the photographic tools I've used over the years, patience has been the most important. I have spent countless hours in meadows, wetlands, forests, and fields watching the light and the birds. In retrospect, each bird, each moment, and each photograph was well worth the wait. I am grateful for this opportunity to share them.

—Jim Roetzel

CEDAR WAXWING (*opposite*)
Cuyahoga Valley National Park, Ohio

The distinctive face mask, eyes, and symmetry of this bird are truly elegant. Typically social birds, they are usually in groups, where behavior such as passing fruit may be observed in between their high-pitched calls.

BIRDS *of* PREY

GOLDEN EAGLE (*previous page*)
Kent State University, Ohio CC

This is "Flash," the Kent State football team mascot. Renowned for their eyesight, talon strength, and wing spans of up to five feet, the Golden Eagle can be found across the Northern Hemisphere.

PEREGRINE FALCON (*above, left*)
Pennsylvania CC

The migratory Peregrine Falcon is capable of flying almost 200 mph when hunting. An endangered species in the 1950s, recovery efforts have increased numbers along mountain ranges, river valleys, and coastlines.

OSPREY (*above, right*)
Everglades National Park, Florida

Diving feet-first, Osprey use their barbed talons to catch their fish. Once in their grip, they adjust the fish so that they face forward, thus causing less drag.

BALD EAGLE
Homer, Alaska

The proud, strong profile, imposing wingspan, and endurance of the Bald Eagle make it the appropriate national emblem of the United States. Found near large bodies of water, Bald Eagles have a wingspan of eight feet and are most prevalent along the east and west coasts of the United States. These beautiful birds of prey build eyries from five to ten feet in width.

NORTHERN HARRIER (*top*)
Huntington Beach, California

The Northern Harrier relies on both hearing and vision to capture prey. Facial feathers are stiff to help transmit sound, and a pronounced "facial disk" is much like that of an owl. It is also known as a "Marsh Hawk."

HARLAN'S HAWK (*bottom, left*)
Vermont CC

Harlan's Hawk is a darker sub-species of the Red-tailed Hawk. Its plumage is blackish with white undersides and a reddish or gray tail. It breeds in Alaska and northwestern Canada, and winters on the southern Great Plains.

GOSHAWK (*bottom, right*)
Vermont CC

Goshawks are likely to be seen within forests, darting through the trees beneath the canopy. They have short, powerful wings and eye tufts which protect them while flying in pursuit of songbirds and squirrels.

RED-TAILED HAWK (*opposite*)
Cuyahoga Valley National Park, Ohio

Widespread across North America, this hawk is a bird of open country. The light variety has a dark patagial mark on its underwing and a gray-red tail, while the dark morphed bird is wholly dark with a brick-red to pink tail.

GREAT HORNED OWLET (*left*)
Venice Beach, Florida

GREAT HORNED OWL (*right*)
Pennsylvania CC

This Great Horned Owlet has yet to develop the adult's prominent ear tufts. The young are similar in coloration to the adults although their barring and dark markings are not as crisp and defined.

Highly recognizable for the feather tufts on its head that resemble horns, the Great Horned Owl's ears are not placed in the same position on either side of its head. The right ear is typically set higher in the skull and at a slightly different angle thus enabling it to better pick up sound. Well known throughout North and South America, it is found from the Arctic tundra to the tropical rainforest.

BURROWING OWLS (*top*)
Cape Coral, Florida

Marked by their prominent white eyebrows and a white patch beneath their beaks, Burrowing Owls have fixed eyes, yet can rotate their heads 270 degrees for peripheral vision. A human can turn their head less than 180 degrees.

BURROWING OWLETS (*bottom*)
Cape Coral, Florida

While the Burrowing Owlet is grayer and tiny, even the adult is a small bird at only ten inches. They can live for ten years, but as ground birds of open grasslands or desert habitats, they are often victims of snakes or coyotes.

SAW-WHET OWL (*left*)
Cuyahoga Valley National Park, Ohio

The Saw-whet's call resembles a saw being sharpened or whetted. Fond of mountainous conifer forests in the eastern and western United States, it will bring one wing across the front of the body as camouflage.

EASTERN SCREECH OWL (*right*)
Vermont CC

Dark streaking on the body helps to camouflage these owls against tree bark. From the Rocky Mountains to the East Coast, they nest in cavities of trees or logs where they store insects, small amphibians, or mice.

GREAT GRAY OWL (*opposite*)
Between Sax and Zim, Minnesota

The Great Gray Owl is the largest owl found in North America. When perched they appear very bulky because of their fluffy plumage. One of the most elusive birds, it is easily identified by its facial disk with two gray concentric circles. Great Gray Owls are found from Alaska, across Canada, down the northern Rocky Mountains, and in northern Minnesota.

AMERICAN KESTREL (*left*)
Vermont CC

Actually a small falcon, the American Kestrel tracks its prey from tall perches, then dives to catch flying insects and small vertebrates. The female has more reddish-white streaked wings and breast, and a multi-barred tail.

SHORT-EARED OWL (*right*)
Mission Mountains, Montana

One of the world's most widespread owls, the Short-eared Owl soars low over fields with flopping wing beats. It has a large, round, facial disk with brown tinges, black around the eyes, and ear tufts that are rarely visible.

BARRED OWL (*opposite*)
Cuyahoga Valley National Park, Ohio

A great hunter, the Barred Owl is able to sneak up on its prey with quiet, soft-feathered wings. However, these feathers limit its ability to swoop and soar. Their distinct call mimics *"Who cooks for you...who cooks for you."*

JUVENILE COOPER'S HAWK (*left*)
Cuyahoga Valley National Park, Ohio

Cooper's Hawks' long tails act as rudders, enabling them to maneuver in wooded areas as they hunt in dense vegetation. Their namesake, William Cooper, was co-founder of the American Museum of Natural History.

BLACK VULTURES (*right*)
Everglades National Park, Florida

With a height of twenty-eight inches and a wingspan of up to five-feet, these vultures are often seen scavenging in dumps or on docks. They nest along rivers or in open areas from South America to the southern United States.

RED-SHOULDERED HAWKS
Everglades National Park, Florida

A forest bird, Red-shouldered Hawks build their nests high in trees near moving water. Found in California and east of the Mississippi, a hawk will stay in one territory for years and return to the same nest each season.

Adults have a brown head, reddish breast, pale belly with reddish bars, and a long tail with narrow white bars. The red "shoulder" is visible when the bird is perched.

MERLIN WINTER FALCON (*left*)
Vermont CC

This accipiter was popular with medieval European falconers hunting small game birds and mammals. In North America, it nests in Canadian grasslands or bogs and migrates to the American West and South.

PRAIRIE FALCON (*right*)
Vermont CC

With slight color variations from the Peregrine, the Prairie Falcon's wings beat quick, strong, and shallow—somewhat mechanically. Nesting on cliff ledges, its habitat includes arid regions and alpine tundra.

SWAINSON'S HAWK (*opposite*)
Tucson, Arizona

Common in the West, the Swainson's Hawk has one of the longest migrations of any American raptor—10,000 kilometers from Canada to Argentina. It can travel nearly 200 kilometers (124 miles) per day.

LARGE LAND BIRDS

WILD TURKEYS (*previous page*)
Bosque del Apache, New Mexico

Wild Turkeys are commonly found in open woodlands. During daylight hours, small, single-sex flocks have been known to search for food in residential areas. These birds can be aggressive and are very fast runners.

SHARP-TAILED GROUSE (*left*)
Devil's Lake State Park, North Dakota

The Sharp-tailed Grouse is an open-prairie bird with a chicken-like appearance. During mating season males establish leks (*courtship grounds*) and defiantly strut in circles with lowered heads and raised feathers.

RUFFED GROUSE (*right*)
Bobcaygeon, Ontario

Widespread throughout North America, the Ruffed Grouse is virtually invisible in the dense growth of its nesting grounds, thanks to its coloring. When startled, they will erupt suddenly from the forest floor.

SPRUCE GROUSE (*opposite*)
Churchill, Manitoba

Spruce Grouse settle in the dense pine and spruce woods of northern-mountain environments. The Spruce Grouse is also known as the "Fool Hen" because it is easily approached and tame enough to handle.

PINK FLAMINGO (*above*)
San Diego Zoo, California CC

The pink hue of this graceful bird is a direct result of its diet, which is high in alpha and beta-carotene from seeds, blue-green algae, and mollusks it filters out of lagoons or mangrove swamp waters. It nests at the water's edge, creating large mounds from mud, stones, and feathers. With colonies that number up to 10,000, a flock of flamingos taking flight is a breathtaking spectacle.

BLUE GROUSE (*opposite*)
National Bison Range, Montana

The plumage of the Blue Grouse is gray-brown, however, males have orange-yellow combs over their eyes and light-gray tail feathers with yellow to red skin, and white neck feathers that they display during courtship. Larger than other typical grouse, they occupy coniferous forests and grasslands in western North America.

AMERICAN CROW (*top*)
Cuyahoga Valley National Park, Ohio

American Crows prefer open areas
with nearby trees such as suburban
and city neighborhoods, parks, and
coastal habitats. Crows sport glossy,
iridescent feathers; young crows have
pink edges to their mouths.

RAVEN (*bottom*)
Yellowstone National Park, Wyoming

In Native-American mythology, the
Raven is typecast as a trickster. Edgar
Allan Poe identified the bird's shriek as
ominous. Perhaps the connotation arises
from its size, iridescent green or purple
sheen, or its omnivorous nature.

GAMBEL'S QUAIL
Bosque del Apache, New Mexico

Gambel's Quails are usually observed in coveys by brush in the deserts of the Southwest, or scurrying surprisingly fast across roads, but flying only if pursued by a predator. Identifiable by their gray plumage, top knots, and scaly undersides, males have copper crowns, black faces, and white eyebrows.

BOBWHITE QUAIL (*top*)
Corkscrew Swamp Sanctuary, Florida

Named for their whistle, "bob-white," this ground-dweller is native to pine or woody growth from the Northeast to Mexico. Popular game birds, they are distinguishable by their black cap and black stripe behind the eye.

WILLOW PTARMIGAN (*bottom, left*)
Churchill, Manitoba

Like many northern Arctic animals, Willow Ptarmigans have separate summer and winter plumage. In summer they are a brownish-red, while in winter, they turn primarily white—a snowy camouflage from predators.

ROCK PTARMIGAN (*bottom, right*)
Nome, Alaska

The Rock Ptarmigan nests above tree line tundra in barren regions of the Yukon and British Columbia. Visually similar to the Willow Ptarmigan, the male has a more prominent, black eye line in winter.

CALIFORNIA QUAIL (*opposite*)
Mount Baldy Area, California

Sometimes called the "Valley Quail," this plump bird has an eye-catching, forward-facing black plume and a black and gray scaled belly. The California Valley Quail is the state bird of California.

SMALLER
OPEN-COUNTRY BIRDS

INDIGO BUNTING (*previous page*)
Cuyahoga Valley National Park, Ohio

The male Indigo Bunting is known for its blue-violet head and bright blue back. Females have a tawny body and blue-edged wings. They migrate after dark, traveling from the Northeast and Southwest to Mexico.

EASTERN BLUEBIRDS (*above*)
Chagrin Falls, Ohio

This lovely thrush is drawn to fences along orchards or farm country. Providing a bluebird house in this setting is likely to draw the bird as well. Note that the Western Bluebird species has a blue throat.

COMMON YELLOWTHROAT WARBLER (*opposite*)
Cuyahoga Valley National Park, Ohio

The strange noise made by whistling and saying the word "pish" is referred to by birders as "pishing." The sound may draw curious songbirds including this Common Yellowthroat Warbler.

CHIPPING SPARROW (*top*)
Cuyahoga Valley National Park, Ohio

The frail nest of the Chipping Sparrow is lined with hair, earning it the name "Hairbird." Nesting in residential gardens or evergreens, it is prolific across the continent and is perhaps most recognized by its trilling chirp.

SWAMP SPARROW (*bottom, left*)
Cuyahoga Valley National Park, Ohio

The Swamp Sparrow is the "dipper" of the sparrow family. Since its diet consists of shallow water invertebrates, this bird can often be seen with its head underwater in an attempt to catch its lunch.

SONG SPARROW (*bottom, right*)
Cuyahoga Valley National Park, Ohio

The Song Sparrow's success with attracting mates or guarding its territory may be directly related to the number and complexity of the male's song parts. Its favorite habitat is a brushy salt marsh area.

SAVANNAH SPARROW (*opposite*)
Cuyahoga Valley National Park, Ohio

Savannah Sparrows were named for the Georgia city where they were first documented. Found in grassy habitats, they differ from other sparrows by their yellow brows, white crown stripe, and short tails.

CLAY-COLORED SPARROW (*left*)
Devil's Lake State Park, North Dakota

The Clay-colored Sparrow summers along the Great Lakes and winters in Texas and Mexico. It is rare on the eastern seaboard. It is distinguished by its conical, dark-tipped beak and buzzing, insect-like song.

TREE SWALLOW (*right*)
Cuyahoga Valley National Park, Ohio

With a diet favoring seeds and berries, the Tree Swallow typically nests in holes made by woodpeckers, near a source of water. With sleek, iridescent, blue-green uppers and a forked tail, it winters farther north than any other swallow.

AMERICAN TREE SPARROW (*opposite*)
Cuyahoga Valley National Park, Ohio

The American Tree Sparrow forages and nests on the ground above northern tree lines. It is able to tolerate sub-zero temperatures if seed is available. During a cold winter, seed-filled feeders can draw these birds in flocks.

GOLDEN-CROWNED
SPARROW (*left*)
Nome, Alaska

Identified by a hint of golden crown, this bird inhabits the Yukon region in the summer then migrates to coastal California. Observers define its three-toned whistle as "Oh dear me."

WHITE-CROWNED SPARROW
(*right*)
Bosque del Apache, New Mexico

This bird acquires its song from the local flock where it is raised, creating multiple dialects of melodies and tone, even within their smaller habitats in Canada and the Southwest.

HOUSE SPARROW (*opposite*)
Cuyahoga Valley National Park, Ohio

One hundred House Sparrows were introduced into Brooklyn during 1851 and 1852. "Dust bathers," they can now be found in residential bird baths from British Columbia to James Bay and south to Panama.

EUROPEAN STARLING (*left*)
Cuyahoga Valley National Park, Ohio

Referred to in the works of William Shakespeare, the European Starling was introduced in New York's Central Park in the late 19th century. It has since become one of the most prolific birds across the continent.

SNOW BUNTING (*right*)
St. Paul Island, Alaska

A circumpolar breeder across the barrens of the Northern Hemisphere, the Snow Bunting migrates to coastlines where it builds nests in rock crevices. It molts from a stark black and white winter plumage to buff and white.

FEMALE HOUSE FINCH (*left*)
Cuyahoga Valley National Park, Ohio

Once a trendy, illegal Mexican import during the 1940s, the House Finch was nicknamed the "Hollywood Finch."

MALE HOUSE FINCH (*right*)
Cuyahoga Valley National Park, Ohio

The House Finch is a seed-eater that frequents bird feeders. It prefers access to woodlands and often nests in conifers. Ornithologists note that the redder the male's breast, the more appeal it seems to have to the female.

COMMON REDPOLL (*top*)
Churchill, Manitoba

Foraging seeds, the Redpoll stores
food in its small throat pouch for
later consumption—important as
seeds are not always readily available
in its most northern winter habitats.

HOARY REDPOLL (*bottom*)
Churchill, Manitoba

Similar to the Common Redpoll, the
rarer Hoary Redpoll has a smaller bill
which gives its face a pushed-in look.
Its downy feathers insulate against
harsh cold, while in mild weather, it
will pluck some of its own feathers.

BOBOLINK (*opposite*)
Cuyahoga Valley National Park, Ohio

Native to open grasslands, the male
Bobolink's plumage is distinctly
unique during mating season, with its
black under body and white back.
Common in the East, it migrates
great distances to South America.

NORTHERN MOCKINGBIRD (*left*)
Everglades National Park, Florida

The repetitive tunes of the Northern Mockingbird mimic other birds and continue into the night throughout the South, the East, and southern Canada. The territorial male will dive at intruders in a quick loop.

PHAINOPEPLA (*right*)
Tucson, Arizona

Native to the Southwest and Mexico, the Phainopepla has glossy dark feathers and a notable crown plume. It fools predators by using other bird's calls and hydrates itself by consuming huge quantities of mistletoe berries.

AMERICAN ROBIN (*top*)
Cuyahoga Valley National Park, Ohio

Known for its large red breast, the American Robin is found throughout the United States and southern Canada. Nesting birds are often seen on lawns where they look (not listen) for worms, insects, and berries. The Robin's two- or three-syllable calls rise and fall, announcing the spring. They can be detected by the presence of broken, pale-blue shells found beneath trees, shrubs, and bushes from their recently hatched chicks.

HOUSE FINCH (*bottom*)
Stow, Ohio

This species will frequent garden bird feeders. But beware, as they can also feed on cultivated buds and fruits, chewing through fruit or flowers to access the seed.

RED-WINGED BLACKBIRD
Cuyahoga Valley National Park, Ohio

A sign of spring, the polygynous male will perch on a marshland cattail to display its red and yellow colors and sing its scratchy "oak-a-lee" song for females. Hatchlings are blind and featherless, yet they manage to leave the nest just ten days after hatching. Identified throughout the continent, large migrating flocks commonly forage grain in harvested fields.

SAY'S PHOEBE (*left*)
Orange County, California

Nesting farther north in Alaska than other flycatchers, the Say's Phoebe is also found from midwestern prairies to eastern California. Its common name honors entomologist Thomas Say's 1819 expedition into the Rockies.

EASTERN PHOEBE (*right*)
Cuyahoga Valley National Park, Ohio

When John James Audubon began banding and tracking American birds around 1840, this wagging-tailed species was reportedly the first to be banded. Male phoebes circle and dive noisily as part of the mating ritual.

BARN SWALLOW (*top*)
Cuyahoga Valley National Park, Ohio

The male Barn Swallow, named for its nesting sites on barn beams and eaves, is marked by its striking, glossy blue color; a long, forked, teal tail; and zigzag flight. Males with the longest tails are popular among females.

WESTERN KINGBIRD (*bottom*)
Chatfield State Park, Colorado

The Western Kingbird has a distinctive gray head, olive-gray body, and pale-yellow to orange underbelly. The male's dramatic courtship behavior involves a twist, a vertical ascent, and a downward spiraling tumble.

EASTERN KINGBIRD (*opposite*)
Floodplain of the Cuyahoga River, Ohio

The Eastern Kingbird builds its sturdy cup nest in trees or on high poles above water that is adjacent to open areas across North America. The male is very territorial, attacking even hawks if threatened.

MOURNING DOVE (*opposite*)
Tucson, Arizona

The Mourning Dove's soft, vibrato cooing is familiar across America. It is the most abundant game bird in North America. More nutritious than cows' milk, the female's regurgitated "pigeon milk" is critical to hatchlings.

MOUNTAIN BLUEBIRD (*top*)
Durango, Colorado

Mountain Bluebirds nest in pairs in decaying trees and trunks with cavities located among forest-fire sites in western North America. If natural sites are sparse, a bluebird will seek out a man-made bird house.

COWBIRD (*bottom*)
Portage Lakes Area, Ohio

Cowbirds do not build nests nor do they raise their young. The female lays her egg in the clutch of another songbird's existing nest. Usually the host bird will hatch, feed, and rear the young Cowbird.

NORTHERN WHEATEAR (*top*)
Nome, Alaska

After nesting in Alaska and Canada, the Northern Wheatear will cross the Bering Strait and Asia to reach African grasslands. The name "wheatear" is a polite English adaptation of "white-arse"—referring to its white rump.

NORTHERN SHRIKE (*bottom, left*)
Newport Beach, California

The Northern Shrike feeds on insects, but it also preys on small birds or mammals. It stores its kill for later consumption, perhaps wise when winters in Canada and the northern United States make food scarce.

YELLOW-HEADED BLACKBIRD (*bottom, right*)
Nine Pipe NWR, Montana

This bird attaches its nest to high marsh reeds, keeping an eye on egg-stealing wrens. It can flock with other blackbird species. The male is marked by a brilliant yellow head, black body, and loud, "rusty-hinge-like" call.

EASTERN MEADOWLARK (*top*)
Cuyahoga Valley National Park, Ohio

Found in grasslands of eastern North America, this bird has a clear, melodious whistle. Not actually a lark, it is closer to the oriole and blackbird families. The female's pointed bill differs from the male's more conical one.

WESTERN MEADOWLARK (*bottom, left*)
Bosque del Apache, New Mexico

Nesting from the Pacific to beyond the Great Lakes, the Western male variety uses a "chase" during pairing. If a male has two mates, one female may initiate the chase; the male will usually chase both females, one at a time.

HORNED LARK (*bottom, right*)
Churchill, Manitoba

The only true lark that is native to all North America, this bird is common in open country. Its most notable features include a black face patch against a pale-yellow throat and horn-like white tufts behind its dark crown.

SMALLER
WOODLAND BIRDS

SMITH'S LONGSPUR (*previous page*)
Churchill, Manitoba

Visually similar to other longspur species, the breeding Smith's Longspur male will mate with multiple females on multiple occasions in an effort to ensure its genetic dominance.

WINTER WREN (*top*)
St. Paul Island, Alaska

Nesting in grassy clumps, Winter Wrens are native to the high cliffs of the Arctic isles, redwood forests of the Pacific Coast, wooded areas of the Rocky Mountains, as well as woodlands of the Appalachian range.

HOUSE WREN (*bottom, left*)
Cuyahoga Valley National Park, Ohio

With a longer body and a stouter bill than the Winter Wren, the House Wren emits a loud alternating high-low pitch of "see-see-see-oodle-oodle" when threatened. It nests in enclosed spaces and garden nest boxes.

CACTUS WREN (*bottom, right*)
McDowell Mountain, Arizona

Arizona's state bird, the Cactus Wren is seven to eight inches in length. Building multiple, protected nests in the niches of large, thorny cacti in the Southwest region, it will live in only one—the rest are decoys.

BROWN THRASHER

Florida

Nesting in thickets and shrubs, this shy bird with its black streaked breast, rufous back, long tail, white wing bars, and yellow eyes, is best detected by its impressive singing that often mimics other species.

FEMALE PURPLE FINCH (*left*)
Cuyahoga Valley National Park, Ohio

The female Purple Finch's coloring is drab compared to her male counterpart's showy raspberry shaded parts. The state bird of New Hampshire, this finch is less prolific than the House Finch.

AMERICAN GOLDFINCH (*right*)
Cuyahoga Valley National Park, Ohio

Familiar across the United States and southern Canada, this gregarious finch issues its mating call "tsee-tsi-tsi-tsit" in June and July. Males exhibit a handsome black cap, wings, and tail, and brilliant lemon-yellow bodies.

GRAY-CROWNED ROSY FINCH (*opposite*)
St. Paul Island, Alaska

Found on barren mountains from Alaska to the Northwest, this is the only finch species with a dark breast coloring. Its rump, wings, and belly are a rose shade; forehead and throat are black; the back of the head is gray.

TUFTED TITMOUSE (*top*)
Cuyahoga Valley National Park, Ohio

Perhaps influenced by global warming, the Tufted Titmouse has been traveling farther north each year. It is discernable by the gray tuft atop its head and a loud whistled song of "peter-peter-peter-peter."

GRAY CATBIRD (*bottom, left*)
Cuyahoga Valley National Park, Ohio

Observed from southwestern Canada to Florida, the Gray Catbird makes its presence known with a cat-like whine issued from dense thickets. Birders who imitate the call usually summon the male of the species.

CHESTNUT-BACKED CHICKADEE (*bottom, right*)
Hurricane Ridge Area, Washington

This bird makes its nests from fur and hair dropped from deer, rabbits, or coyotes. Nests are found in coniferous or deciduous tree cavities from the central coast of California to Alaska.

BLACK-CAPPED CHICKADEE (*opposite*)
Cuyahoga Valley National Park, Ohio

Across North America, this relatively tame, backyard bird has been known to take seed from an open hand. The distinct "chick-a-dee-dee" can vary, thus conveying different messages.

GREAT-CRESTED FLYCATCHER (*opposite*)
Southwest Adirondacks, New York

This male's bright yellow belly is hidden so that its coloring camouflages it against its snake-skin-lined nest in a hollowed tree. Sightings require following its strong, rising "wee-eep" call.

ACADIAN FLYCATCHER (*left*)
Cuyahoga Valley National Park, Ohio

The Acadian Flycatcher nests on dense, coniferous, forest floors. It is found from the southeastern Dakotas to New England and the Southeast. Shy and quiet in its movement, it is a challenging bird to view.

WILLOW FLYCATCHER (*right*)
Cuyahoga Valley National Park, Ohio

All flycatchers return to their previous year's nest in wet, brushy, territory across the United States and southern Canada. A Willow Flycatcher that finds cowbird eggs in a nest will build a new nest directly on top of the old one.

BLUE-GRAY GNATCATCHER (*left*)
Brazos Bend State Park, Texas

The Blue-gray Gnatcatcher is fearless when protecting its nest in deciduous woodlands or stream-side thickets. Found from California to New Hampshire and south to Texas, it can attack birds three times its size.

LAPLAND LONGSPUR (*right*)
Nome, Alaska

"Longspur" refers to this bird's hind toe claw. It breeds during the constant summer daylight in the most northern Arctic regions. Winter flocks can number up to several million birds.

BALTIMORE ORIOLE (*opposite*)
Cuyahoga Valley National Park, Ohio

Maryland's state bird, the Baltimore Oriole is easily identified by its bright orange and black coloring. Its gray, tube-like nest is found in deciduous trees and woods.

CURVED-BILLED THRASHER (*top*)
Phoenix, Arizona

OREGON JUNCO (*bottom*)
California

Stick nests of the Curved-billed Thrasher are located in the center of dense, thorny vegetation in southwestern deserts. The bird's double whistle "whit-wheet" is very distinct from any other thrasher species.

A medium-sized sparrow, the Oregon Junco is known as a "snowbird." It summers throughout Alaska, Canada, and mountainous regions of the United States, then moves to more southern elevations in winter.

RUFOUS-SIDED TOWHEE
Cuyahoga Valley National Park, Ohio

While the head and upper body are brown on the female, both sexes exhibit reddish-brown sides and a white belly. This species is sometimes referred to as a "chewink" after the sound of its most common call.

DARK-EYED JUNCO (*above*)
Cuyahoga Valley National Park, Ohio

Juncos typically build ground nests on banks with overhanging tree roots or rock ledges. With fifteen different varieties, Dark-eyed Juncos are the most common feeder-birds across the continent in winter.

WHITE-BREASTED NUTHATCH (*opposite*)
Cuyahoga Valley National Park, Ohio

The White-breasted Nuthatch exhibits unusual behavior—it feeds by hopping along tree trunks and branches, often hanging upside down. It will jam a nut into a tree and hammer it open with its bill. Defending its territory, it will sweep a piece of fur or vegetation around its nest cavity, masking its own scent from possible predators.

ROSE-BREASTED GROSBEAK (*opposite*)
Cuyahoga Valley National Park, Ohio

Observed in temperate climates throughout North America in the summer, the Rose-breasted Grosbeak winters in southern Mexico. Its song is similar to the American Robin, only sweeter and more melodic, while its squeaky "eek-eek" call sounds like rubber soles on a hardwood floor. Its nest of grass and twigs is so delicate that the eggs may often be seen through its netting.

EVENING GROSBEAK (*above*)
Cuyahoga Valley National Park, Ohio

Sighted throughout North America, this bird will irrupt across the United States and Canada based upon food supplies. Drawn to sunflower seed, watch for its brown head and nape, and bright yellow brow and back.

BROAD-TAILED
HUMMINGBIRD (*left*)
Durango, Colorado

Seen from Idaho to the Rockies, this bird's wings produce a distinct trilling noise during flight. Both sexes have iridescent green backs and crowns, while the male has a bright red throat patch.

RUFOUS HUMMINGBIRD (*right*)
Durango, Colorado

Small and very maneuverable, this hummingbird may return annually to the same location, even the same feeder. An elegant addition to any garden, the male has an orange back, body, and tail with pointed black tip, and a red throat. The female exhibits a white throat with some red; an iridescent black and green head and back; and an orange, green, and black tail with rounded white tips.

RUBY-THROATED HUMMINGBIRD (*top*)
Magee Marsh, Ohio

Ruby-throats adapt to humans quickly and are often drawn to the color red. Most common in the eastern United States, the male has a bright red gorget; the female has a white-tipped tail.

ANNA'S HUMMINGBIRD (*bottom*)
Newport Beach, California

Seen from California, north to Alaska and east to the Mississippi, females build nests from plant down and spider webs. The male's courtship involves hovering high, a squeeky warble, and diving down in a big arc.

WHITE-EYED VIREO (*top*)
Magee Marsh, Ohio

The White-eyed Vireo's white and black eyes stand out against its yellow mask and gray crown. A 400,000 year-old fossil of this specific species was identified in Florida.

RED-EYED VIREO (*bottom, left*)
Southwest Adirondacks, New York

This vireo is abundant in the deciduous trees of eastern forests in the summer. Its call, one of the few heard on a hot mid-day, is a series of abrupt, two- and three-note whistles that are repeated as often as forty times a minute.

BLUE-HEADED VIREO AND YOUNG COWBIRD (*bottom, right*)
Cuyahoga Valley National Park, Ohio

Easily identified by its blue-gray head, dark-brown eyes, and contrasting white spectacles, the Blue-head breeds across the Canadian provinces, south through the Midwest, and the Carolinas.

BLUE-HEADED VIREO (*opposite*)
Cuyahoga Valley National Park, Ohio

Of the three different "Solitary Vireo" species, the Blue-headed Vireo is the most colorful. It has the easternmost habitat and summers from Alberta to Newfoundland, migrating south along the Gulf and the Southeast coasts.

OVENBIRD (*top*)
Acadia National Park, Maine

The Ovenbird's name is derived from its domed nest with a side entrance resembling a Dutch oven. Common from the Midwest to eastern forests, male birds may sing alternately to each other for long periods.

WARBLING VIREO (*bottom*)
South Dakota

This bird's preferred nesting habitats include seasonal woodlands or groves near streams, from British Columbia to New Brunswick and south to Virginia. More easily heard than seen, its rapid twitter ends on a high-pitched note.

VEERY (*opposite*)
Cuyahoga Valley National Park, Ohio

The Veery is partial to damp, boggy, deciduous woodlands. Its call is a lovely, flute-like, falling spiral song. Its common "vee-er" call gives this bird its name.

CHESTNUT-SIDED WARBLER (*top*)
Cuyahoga Valley National Park, Ohio

This is the only warbler species that displays a greenish-yellow cap, a white breast, and distinctive reddish streaks down its sides. The male warbler's mating song is an emphatically accented "pleased-to-MEETCHA."

HOODED WARBLER (*bottom, left*)
Cuyahoga Valley National Park, Ohio

From Wisconsin to the Gulf Coast, Hooded Warblers prefer shaded, separate-sex habitats. The male, with a yellow face and a black hood and collar, prefers mature under-forests, while hoodless females like wooded swamps.

WESTERN PALM WARBLER
(*bottom, right*)
Venice, Florida

All Palm Warblers wag their rumps, emphasizing their yellow under-tails. They will migrate to Florida and the Caribbean in the winter but will summer all the way into northern Canada.

BAY-BREASTED WARBLER
Magee Marsh, Ohio

At six inches, this large warbler nests in stands of mature firs and hemlock throughout eastern Canada, primarily from Ottawa and into Maine. It will only wag its tail while feeding.

MAGNOLIA WARBLER (*top*)
Magee Marsh, Ohio

First classified from a sighting in a Mississippi Magnolia tree, this bird's breeding plumage is distinctive with its bold black and white facial pattern, gray cap, and wings with a white patch. The female is more muted.

BLUE-WINGED WARBLER (*bottom*)
Cuyahoga Valley National Park, Ohio

As shrubby, second-growth, man-made habitats are developed, the Blue-winged Warbler population decreases, especially in the Northeast. In a survival effort, the Blue-winged hybridizes with the Golden-winged.

YELLOW WARBLER (*opposite*)
Cuyahoga Valley National Park, Ohio

The male Yellow Warbler is identified by its golden-yellow plumage and rusty streaks on his breast. With varieties that range from northern Canada to Panama, this warbler favors the multi-floral rose as a nesting site.

HERMIT THRUSH (*top*)
Acadia National Park, Maine

Of several spot-breasted thrushes seen from Alaska, south to coastal California, and east through the Maritimes, the Hermit Thrush has the darkest, most distinct marks. It nests in the shrubs of conifer forests in higher elevations.

SCARLET TANAGER (*bottom, left*)
Cuyahoga Valley National Park, Ohio

Scarlet Tanagers might be referred to as "neck strainers"; birders must often look straight up into the top of the forest canopy to see them. Viewed mostly in the Northeast, tanagers are sensitive to forest fragmentation.

WHITE-THROATED SPARROW
(*bottom, right*)
Cuyahoga Valley National Park, Ohio

Common in the Northeast, this bird's white throat patch and yellow spots are distinctive. There are two morphs with white or tan crowns. They usually mate with the opposite color form.

EASTERN TOWHEE (*opposite*)
Cuyahoga Valley National Park, Ohio

The Eastern Towhee's delightful song has several notes followed by a trilled "drink-your-teeeee." Part of the sparrow family, Eastern Towhees nest in low bushes or grasses from New England to Virginia and the Midwest.

PURPLE MARTINS (*left*)
Buckhorn, Ontario

Martins generally rely on man-made nesting sites including clay pots, hollowed gourds, and multi-holed bird houses. Purple Martins are actually dark steel-blue with brown-black wings; the female is browner.

GREAT-TAILED GRACKLE
(*top, right*)
Anahuac National Wildlife Refuge, Texas

In Central America, large, noisy grackle roosts are frequently found in small town plazas. Their territorial challenges with other birds and sharp barks and whistles can be annoying.

BOAT-TAILED GRACKLE
(*bottom, right*)
Florida

The male Boat-tailed Grackle is about four inches longer than the Common Grackle. Its longer, wider, "V"-shaped tail creases to form the appearance of a boat's keel when the bird is in flight.

COMMON GRACKLE
Cuyahoga Valley National Park, Ohio

Part of the same family as orioles, blackbirds, and cowbirds, the Common Grackle is regularly seen across the Midwest and along the Atlantic Coast. An opportunistic feeder, grackles will damage seedling crops or brazenly snatch crumbs at outdoor cafes, leaving quite a mess. During evening stops, thousands of the birds may be seen—as well as heard—roosting together in a single tree.

RED-BELLIED WOODPECKER (*left*)
Everglades National Park, Florida

DOWNY WOODPECKER (*right*)
Cuyahoga Valley National Park, Ohio

Ironically, the Red-bellied Woodpecker of the Southeast has only a
touch of red on its white underside,
while its brilliant red crown and hind
neck contrast with the black-and-
white bars on its back and wings.

The most common American woodpecker, the Downy is found throughout North America, from Alaska to
Florida. It thrives in a variety of habitats from wilderness forests to urban
parks or backyard bird feeders.

PILEATED WOODPECKER (*left*)
Cuyahoga Valley National Park, Ohio

At sixteen to nineteen inches in length, the Pileated Woodpecker is the largest woodpecker found in North America. It makes its presence known with a loud hammering "kuk-kuk-kuk" call and large holes left in dead trees.

HAIRY WOODPECKER (*right*)
Cuyahoga Valley National Park, Ohio

Across North America, the Hairy Woodpecker is easily recognized by its white body with contrasting black tail, wings with white bands, a black mask, and a red patch on the back of its head. The female's head patch is black.

RED-HEADED WOODPECKER (*left*)
Cuyahoga Valley National Park, Ohio

One of the most aggressive and omnivorous woodpeckers, the Red-headed species will attack rivals and destroy their nests and eggs. It breeds in deciduous woodlands, preferring areas of dead or recently burnt trees.

ACORN WOODPECKER (*right*)
California

Drilling up to 50,000 holes in a single tree or pole to store their acorns, an extended family of Acorn Wood-peckers nests as a team to protect their cache. They make a distinct loud tapping and "waka-waka-waka" call.

NORTHERN FLICKER (*opposite*)
Noble County, Ohio

The male Northern Flicker is the yellow-shafted form common to eastern and northern regions. The red-shafted form is a western bird. A hammering wood-pecker, both forms prefer to lap up ground ants using their barbed tongues.

STELLER'S JAY (*opposite*)
Mount Rainier National Park, Washington

Steller's Jays are common in coniferous forests from Alaska, along the Rockies, to mountainous areas of lower Central America. They often imitate the cry of the Red-tailed Hawk to clear competition from a feeding area.

BLUE JAY (*left*)
Cuyahoga Valley National Park, Ohio

The Blue Jay is recognized by its loud cackling "jay jay" calls and melodious, whistling song, as well as its bright blue crown, back, and barred wings. Its territorial aggression is evident in parks and residential areas.

NORTHERN CARDINAL (*right*)
Cuyahoga Valley National Park, Ohio

The official bird of seven states, the male has beautiful red plumage while the female is tan with red highlights. Cardinals are common in the Midwest, New York, and New England. They winter in Mexico.

FLORIDA SCRUB JAY (*left*)
Florida

While this adult jay has bright blue shades, the youngling (seen here) bears lighter browns and blues. Exclusive to Florida, it is an endangered species due to the reduction of the "scrub" habitat along Florida's coastal regions.

WESTERN SCRUB JAY (*right*)
California

This brightly-colored Scrub Jay of the American West is nonmigratory, remaining in lowlands and suburban areas. Those nesting near oaks will bury caches of seeds or bugs, hiding them from other jays.

GRAY JAY (*opposite*)
Churchill, Manitoba

Like a large chickadee and friendly to the point of stealing food from human hands, this jay will brazenly raid forested campsites, from Alaska to Labrador and across the northern United States.

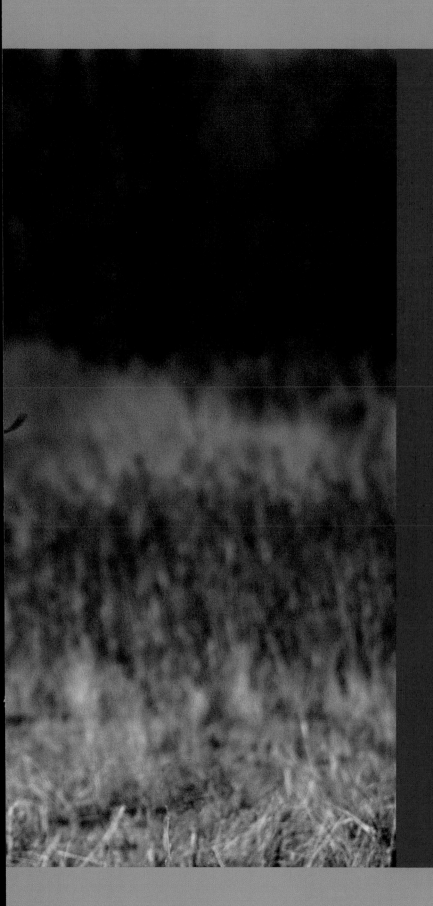

DUCK-LIKE BIRDS

SNOW GEESE (*previous page*)
Bosque del Apache, New Mexico

Presenting either an all-white body or a gray-brown body with a white head, Snow Geese migrate in large, bunched flocks or in broad "U" formations across Pacific coastal areas to the Rockies and along coastal Texas.

PACIFIC LOON (*top*)
Churchill, Manitoba

The Pacific Loon nests on lakeside platforms of roots and mud in Alaska and northern Canada. It winters at sea, mainly on the Pacific Coast, or on large lakes where it wails a high-pitched warble.

COMMON LOON (*bottom*)
Cleveland, Ohio

A symbol of peaceful wilderness, this loon's eerie, piercing call echoes across Canadian lakes throughout the breeding season. The male measures up to three feet from its black head to its checkered black-and-white mantle.

WOOD DUCKS (*opposite*)
Cleveland, Ohio

Though exquisitely colored, the male Wood Duck still relies on courtship behavior. His impressive wing displays, thin, rising and falling "zeet-like" whistle, and mutual kiss-like preening are all necessary to win his mate.

FEMALE WOOD DUCK

Cuyahoga Valley National Park, Ohio

Less colorful than her male counterpart, the female Wood Duck's coloring provides camouflage. Her crest and
cheek are gray; her breast is a mottled
white-brown; and her upper parts are
olive-gray with a metallic sheen.

MALE WOOD DUCK (*top*)
Cleveland, Ohio

Striking in appearance, the male is considered one of the most beautiful of all ducks. The Wood Duck nests in trees close to marshy areas, especially where nest boxes are provided.

MALLARD DRAKE (*bottom, left*)
Cleveland, Ohio

The Mallard breeds in temperate and subtropical North America, migrating as far south as Central America. The northernmost birds are larger, reflecting Allen's rule that climate temperatures affect size.

FEMALE MALLARD (*bottom, right*)
Castalia, Ohio

The female Mallard emits a cliché "quack" call. She protects her feathers with frequent preening—squeezing oil from a gland at the base of the tail onto her bill and across her plumage which insulates from environmental pollutants.

MASKED DUCK (*top, left*)
Brazos Bend State Park, Texas

A species known for its stiff tail held upright, breeding males have a rust-colored body with a black face. They nest along secluded mangroves or marshy coastlines from Texas through Mexico and sometimes Florida.

BUFFLEHEAD (*bottom, left*)
Huntington Beach, California

The smallest diving duck in North America, the Bufflehead nests almost exclusively in holes excavated by Northern Flickers. This duck is identified by its large bulbous head and white coloring behind the eye.

AMERICAN COOT (*right*)
Florida

The American Coot's slate-gray plumage and white chicken-like beak distinguish this rail from actual duck species. While a swimmer, it does not have webbed feet, instead it has lobes between its toes that aid in paddling.

AMERICAN BLACK DUCK/MALLARD HYBRID
Castalia, Ohio

The American Black Duck often cross-breeds with captive-bred mallards that now outnumber, and often overtake, breeding habitats. While the pure American Black has a dark yellow beak, black-brown coloring that is lighter in the head to neck, and a dark cap and eye line, the hybrid has the Mallard's notable iridescent green in its cap. Both males have a bright purple speculum and white underwing linings.

RED-THROATED LOON (*opposite*)
Nome, Alaska

This unique loon species of Canadian lakes and Arctic coasts is small in size and is able to take flight from a small land area. It searches for fish beyond its nesting site and refuses duckling transport on its back.

PINTAIL (*top*)
Newport Beach, California

The Northern Pintail has a long, white neck and bluish bill. The drake's plumage includes a velvet-brown head, and a splendid combination of black, tan, and gray patches with bronze bands along the wings.

BLACK MALLARD HYBRID
(*bottom, left*)
Cleveland, Ohio

Hybrid Mallard and Black Ducks, while often darker than Mallards, may take on any one of the Mallard's visual attributes, making some hybrids hard to identify or differentiate.

FEMALE REDHEAD DUCK
(*bottom, right*)
Newport Beach, California

Fast becoming one of North America's rarest species of duck, the female is marked with gray and brown plumage and a bluish-gray bill. They are known to lay their eggs in other ducks nests.

CANADA GOOSE

Cuyahoga Valley National Park, Ohio

The most familiar and widespread goose in North America, migrating flocks of Canada Geese are lovely sights throughout the fall across America and Canada. Canada Geese often return annually to familiar spots only to find residential or urban development where their presence is perceived as a nuisance due to their large size, noisy honking, and copious calling cards.

FEMALE RING-NECKED DUCK (*top*)
Cleveland, Ohio

Found in smaller ponds across the continent's temperate regions, this duck's quiet call and rarely visible violet neck-ring require special birding skills. Ring-necks are usually identified by their size and the white ring around their bills.

GREATER SCAUP (*bottom*)
Churchill, Manitoba

Among duck hunters, this bird is known as a "blue-bill." Its common name is probably derived from the bird's infrequent "scaup scaup" call. The scaup's habitat and range are similar to the Ring-necked Duck.

NORTHERN SHOVELER (*top*)
High Island Area, Texas

The Northern Shoveler is named for its spoon-shaped bill that is fringed with bristles, allowing it to strain food from mud and water.

RUDDY DUCK (*bottom*)
Phoenix, Arizona

The Ruddy Duck is found along the coasts of the Southeast, Gulf of Mexico, and the Northwest in winter and the Canadian Rockies in summer. One of the stiff-tailed ducks, the male holds its tail up for courtship displays.

BLUE-WINGED TEAL (*opposite*)
Winnie, Texas

Viewed only in flight, powder-blue underwings give this duck its name. The Blue-winged Teal breeds across northern and central North America and is mostly seen in shallow ponds.

AMERICAN WIDGEON (*top*)
Castalia, Ohio

Also known as the "Baldpate" because of its white forehead, this widgeon breeds in the Northwest but migrates throughout the rest of the continent. A dabbler, its diet is mostly vegetation from ponds and fields.

SURF SCOOTER (*bottom, left*)
Huntington Beach, California

This large sea duck breeds in Canada and Alaska and winters on the Pacific and Atlantic coasts. Its dramatic bill is yellow with white, red, and black markings, while the female's bill is blue-black.

CINNAMON TEAL (*bottom, right*)
Newport Beach, California

The Cinnamon Teal breeds in both western North America and South America. Spotting a nest is difficult, as it is concealed below matted, dead plant-life. The female accesses the nest via tunnels in the vegetation.

TRUMPETER SWAN

Yellowstone National Park, Wyoming

Pure white with a black bill and mask, up to five feet in length, and with an impressive wing-span of over six feet, the Trumpeter Swan is the largest waterfowl in North America. It nests in freshwater from Alaska to western South Dakota and Nebraska, Minnesota, Wisconsin, and Michigan. It then migrates to the Southwest's lakes and streams, feeding on vegetation and grains. Once mated, these graceful swans usually remain together for life.

CLARK'S GREBE (*top*)
Huntington Beach, California

Recognized by its shrill whistle and wavy croak, the Clark's Grebe has a bill that is less green than the Western Grebe. Its feet are far back on the body and a small lobe on its hind toe reduces drag and increases speed.

RED-NECKED GREBE (*bottom, left*)
Anchorage, Alaska

The male Red-necked Grebe has a white chin, black crown, and rufous neck during winter breeding. Both male and female build a floating, grassy nest that they anchor to emergent grasses in marshy ponds.

HORNED GREBE (*bottom, right*)
Manitoba

This bird's yellow horned brows are raised and lowered during mating rituals in northwestern Canada. At rest, the grebe lays its neck on its back with one foot tucked up under a wing, while using the other as a rudder.

YOUNG PIED-BILLED GREBE
Manitoba

The Pied-billed Grebe is common throughout North America. Although it can fly, it prefers to escape predators by diving, thus its nickname "Hell-diver." While breeding, it has a black throat and a short, black-ringed bill.

DOUBLE-CRESTED
CORMORANT (*left*)
Ding Darling NWR, Florida

The Double-crested Cormorant is the most numerous and widespread cormorant found in North America. They are often seen drying their wings by stretching them out in the sun.

ANHINGA (*right, and opposite*)
Everglades National Park, Florida

Known as the "snake bird," this bird is sometimes mistaken for a snake when surfacing head-first from a dive. From Latin America to North Carolina, it feeds by spearing fish with its long serrated bill. Lacking oil glands for waterproofing its feathers, it spreads its wings to dry. The male (right) has greenish-black plumage and silver-gray wings edged with long white plumes.

PURPLE GALLINULE (*left*)
Everglades National Park, Florida

Seen in wetlands from Florida to Central America, this gallinule has a purple-blue head, neck, and underside; a green back; and yellow legs with extremely long toes that aid in walking on top of floating vegetation.

COMMON MOORHEN (*right*)
Brazos Bend State Park, Texas

A member of the rail family, this bird inhabits marshes and ponds from eastern Canada and the Great Lakes, to Chile. Long toes enable it to walk on mud and floating vegetation where it will attach its nest and feed on bugs.

THICK-BILLED MURRES (*opposite*)
St. Paul Island, Alaska

Also known as "Brünnich's Guillemot," colonies of murres breed in coastal areas along Arctic cliffs, nesting directly on a ledge. Like other auks, they use their small wings to swim underwater for up to four minutes.

PARAKEET AUKLETS (*opposite*)
St. Paul Island, Alaska

Parakeet Auklets breed along frigid offshore islands in Alaska. Their territories extend only a few feet beyond a nest until birds move south for the winter. As seen opposite, breeding auks "bill" and "duet" with each other.

CRESTED AUKLET (*left*)
St. Paul Island, Alaska

Crested Auklets nest in huge colonies of up to a million birds. Feathers above the orange beak are bristly. A tangerine-like odor that is emitted during breeding will stave off fox, raven, and gull predators.

LEAST AUKLET (*right*)
St. Paul Island, Alaska

Abundant in North America, Least Auklets winter onshore but nest along rocky coasts of the Aleutians. Their nests are often robbed by other auklets. Artic fox and rats have reduced their numbers as well.

BLACK-BELLIED WHISTLING
DUCK (*top*)

Brazos Bend State Park, Texas

Striking in its chestnut plumage, this
"Tree Duck" nests in coastal tree cavities
from Louisiana to South America. By
choosing a long-term mate, its behavior is more like a goose than a duck.

LIGHT-FOOTED CLAPPER RAIL
(*bottom, left*)

Huntington Beach, California

This rail, found along the coast of
southern California, is one of twenty
Clapper Rail species found in the
Americas. Visible at high tide, its coloring blends into the dense marsh.

VIRGINIA RAIL (*bottom, right*)

Cuyahoga Valley National Park, Ohio

With long toes, this bird forages head
first through marshy areas along the
United States and Mexican coastlines
as well as swamps across the northern
United States and Canada. It deters
predators by building multiple nests.

HORNED PUFFIN
St. Paul Island, Alaska

Horned Puffins inhabit sea cliffs or
rocky islands off the Alaskan coast and
British Columbia. Their large bills
allow them to deliver several fish at a
time to their young. They winter on
the open sea, offshore from their nests.

SORA (*top, left*)
Newport Beach, California

Once known as the Sora Rail, this sometime aviator flies straight with dangling legs then drops into the water. Its whinnying call is heard in marshy areas, although it is difficult to see among briars, reeds, and cattails.

CLAPPER RAIL (*bottom, left*)
Merritt Island NWR, Florida

The Clapper Rail resides in saltwater marshes along the Atlantic, Gulf, and California coasts. Eastern birds have a buff breast, while western birds are chestnut. A downward-curved bill aids in nabbing sea life and insects.

RED-FACED CORMORANT (*right*)
St. Paul Island, Alaska

The male's eye-catching mating plumage includes a dark tuft; an iridescent black, green, and violet back; a double crest of white plumes on the flanks, neck and rump; a blue-based bill; and its namesake red mask.

FEMALE RED-BREASTED MERGANSER (*opposite*)
Ding Darling NWR, Florida

At over twenty-four inches, the male has a cat-like mating call that is answered by the female's harsh "gruk." It nests in northern Canada and Alaska, farther north than other mergansers.

GULL-LIKE BIRDS

BLACK-LEGGED KITTIWAKE
(*previous page*)
Bird Rock, Newfoundland

Identified by its white and gray body, black-tipped wings, and yellow bill, this cliff-nesting gull generally spends the winter on the open ocean where it feeds on small fish and plankton.

MEW GULL (*top*)
Anchorage, Alaska

The smallest white-headed gull in North America, its "mew" call, size, and yellow parts differentiate it from other gulls along the seacoast and marshy grasslands from Alaska to coastal Washington.

MEW GULL HATCHLINGS (*bottom*)
Anchorage, Alaska

In their first few days, these fluffy little brindle patterned chicks with pink beaks will be fed insects and small fish. Later, they will begin to forage for bugs and master fishing with the essential plunge-dive.

ARCTIC TERN (*opposite*)
Churchill, Manitoba

This bird has the longest migration of any animal. From the Canadian Arctic it flies to Antarctica and back, spending the entire winter at sea. When fishing, it will fly into the wind, hover, sight its prey, and then dive.

NORTHERN GANNET (*top*)
Bird Rock, Newfoundland

From the Atlantic Coast to the North
Sea, gannet colonies nest on cliffs or
rocky islands. They have dramatic
black-tipped wings that span up to
five feet. A mating pair will "bill" and
preen their long necks.

HERRING GULL EGGS (*bottom*)
Trinity, Newfoundland

Herring Gulls build nests of seaweeds
and grasses on remote, rocky coastal
ground. They defend their nests
aggressively against foxes, birds of
prey, or humans by darting and emit-
ting a high-pitched, yodel-like call.

HERRING GULL (*opposite*)
Trinity, Newfoundland

Across North America, the white,
gray, and black feathers, along with
the yellow bill generically define a
seagull. Scavengers, these fish lovers
also raid trash cans and will even grab
a sandwich from a beach-goer's hand.

PARASITIC JAEGER (*top*)
Churchill, Manitoba

This jaeger breeds in Arctic regions of
the Alaskan coast and Canada, migrating to the Tropics in winter. They
will swoop upon terns and gulls,
stealing their fish. The farthest tundra
dwellers hunt rodents, birds, and fish.

LAUGHING GULL (*bottom*)
Sanibel Causeway, Florida

Named for its human-like call, this
small gull is identified by its black head.
In the 19th century, its plumes were
hunted and eggs harvested to near
extinction. Today, it is abundant along
the southern Atlantic and Gulf coasts.

BONAPARTE'S GULL (*opposite*)
Churchill, Manitoba

A small, dove-like bird, this gull has a
striking black head with white crescents
behind the eyes, along with a gray back,
and wings patched in white. Its common name honors 19th-century orni-
thologist, Charles Lucien Bonaparte.

AMERICAN WHITE PELICAN (*top*)
Placida, Florida

Up to fifty inches in length and with a wingspan that can exceed ten feet, White Pelicans are excellent surface fishers. Multiple birds will herd fish in front of them, submerge their heads, and scoop up their catch.

HEERMANN'S GULL (*bottom, left*)
San Diego, California

Masters of stealing fish from Brown Pelicans, the Heermann's is the only gull that breeds south on the offshore islands of western Mexico and California and then winters farther north than its nesting area.

BLACK SKIMMER (*bottom, right*)
Ding Darling NWR, Florida

The Black Skimmer's eye has cat-like vertical pupils. The lower beak section is longer than the upper, allowing it to "skim" for fish. It breeds along coastal California and from Massachusetts to Texas.

BROWN PELICAN (*opposite*)
San Diego, California

Upon catching fish in its three-gallon pouch, the Brown Pelican is often pestered by thieving gulls perched on its back, looking to steal a meal. An endangered species, pollutants cause soft egg shells that are easily broken.

LARGE
WADING BIRDS

SANDHILL CRANES (*previous page*)
Bosque del Apache, New Mexico

This very large long-necked bird flies with its neck extended and its legs trailing behind it. Adult Sandhills are gray with a patch of red on their forehead and they have a long, pointed bill.

GREAT EGRET (*top*)
Venice, Florida

The symbol of the National Audubon Society, the Great Egret was nearly extinct around 1900 from plume hunting for hats. Second only in size to the Great Blue Heron, this egret has a lifespan of up to twenty-three years.

CATTLE EGRET (*bottom*)
Venice, Florida

The Cattle Egret is native to dry habitats of Africa and Asia, only reaching the Americas in the late 19th century. Its name comes from perching on the backs of cattle where it eats the insects that buzz around them.

SNOWY EGRET (*opposite*)
Ding Darling NWR, Florida

Once hunted for its lace-like plumes, the Snowy Egret continues to be protected from extinction. This small, delicate heron is identified by its yellow face and feet, thin black bill, and entirely white plumage.

LITTLE GREEN HERON (*top*)
Cuyahoga Valley National Park, Ohio

The bluish-green gloss of the Little Green Heron's back feathers gleem in the sunlight. A smaller heron at fourteen inches in length, its fishing strategy is rare among birds; it employs bait to attract and catch small fish.

RUDDY TURNSTONE (*bottom*)
Nome, Alaska

A true forager, the Ruddy Turnstone will overturn stones and other objects in search of insects and invertebrates. The male will scrape the ground as part of a courtship ritual and nesting site selection process.

GLOSSY IBIS (*opposite*)
Florida

Native to Africa, the Glossy Ibis came to inland wetlands of the Americas only decades ago. Black at first glance, it is a lustrous purple-red, with iridescent green wings and tail, and a long, gracefully-curved bill.

YELLOW-CROWNED NIGHT HERON (*left*)
Ding Darling NWR, Florida

With a high, squawking bark, blue-gray plumage, and yellow crown, this heron beckons a mate. It breeds along wooded wetlands from Connecticut to the Gulf and up the Mississippi.

BLACK-CROWNED NIGHT HERON (*right*)
Winnipeg, Canada

The stocky Black-crowned Night Heron breeds across southern Canada. It feeds at dusk or early morning in marshes and lakes, catching fish to be used as surface bait for larger fish.

LITTLE BLUE HERON (*opposite*)
Everglades National Park, Florida

Standing only about two feet, the Little Blue Herron is all white until it becomes an adult. Both sexes have slate-blue feathers with a maroon neck and head and are found in fresh-water swamps, lagoons, and coastal thickets.

AMERICAN BITTERN
Brazos Bend State Park, Texas

Almost three feet tall, with light and dark brown streaks, an American Bittern stands perfectly still with its head pointing up so as to blend in with the marsh vegetation, making it practically impossible to see. It is most obvious by its loud, deep, guttural "oong-a-choonk" call.

LEAST BITTERN (*left*)
Anuahc National Wildlife Refuge, Texas

Smaller and with softer coloring than the American Bittern, the Least Bittern is also a master of camouflage yet has a less boisterous "coo." Straddling reeds, it can feed in water too deep for wading.

ROSEATE SPOONBILL (*right*)
Everglades National Parks, Florida

A noisy shrimp-eater, the Roseate Spoonbill swings its long, submerged bill back and forth and shuts it instinctively when food enters. It breeds along mangroves in coastal Texas, Louisiana, and southern Florida.

HUDSONIAN GODWIT (*top*)
Churchill, Manitoba

A large shorebird, the Hudsonian Godwit is marked by a relatively long, upturned reddish bill. After breeding in the remote north, it migrates several thousand miles, non-stop, from the Subarctic to southern South America.

WHITE IBIS (*bottom*)
Sanibel Island, Florida

The White Ibis nests in huge colonies in fresh-water marshes or along the coast from Virginia to Florida. They are identified by their long, down-curved red bill. Their long, gray legs turn red during breeding season.

WOOD STORK (*opposite*)
Myakka River State Park, Florida

Prehistoric in appearance, Wood Storks are bald with heavy, dark bills, have a pinkish sheen on their white wings, and stand three feet tall. Four-foot-wide nests are built in cypress trees from South Carolina through Florida.

GREEN-BACKED HERON (*top, left*)
Everglades National Park, Florida

Using insects and feathers as bait,
the Green-backed Heron will wait
motionless, perched on low lying
mangroves, waiting to ambush its
prey of fish, frogs, or crabs.

LIMPKIN (*bottom, left*)
Myakka River State Park, Florida

The Limpkin feeds on apple snails or
shellfish extracted from their shells
with its long, slightly curved bill. Its
screaming cry of "ow, ow, ow, ow, ow"
is prominent across marshlands of
Florida and Honduras.

TRI-COLORED HERON (*right*)
Ding Darling NWR, Florida

At a length of twenty-two inches, this
heron holds its head in an "S-curve"
at rest. During breeding, the male
exhibits long blue or buff plumes
about the head, neck, and back.

GREAT BLUE HERON (*opposite*)
Venice Rookery, Florida

The Great Blue Heron is the largest
heron species on the continent. Its
breeding grounds or "heronries" are
comprised of nests of sticks built
high in trees across North American
wetlands.

SHORE BIRDS

SPOTTED SANDPIPER (*previous page*)
Cuyahoga Valley National Park, Ohio

A rarity, the female Spotted Sandpiper builds ground nests and defends the territory rather than the male. After mating, she will lay eggs that are often fathered by a different male, having saved an earlier mate's sperm.

ROCK SANDPIPER (*top*)
St. Paul Island, Alaska

The heavily-camouflaged Rock Sandpiper roosts along the northern tundra coasts of Alaska and regional islands. It nests on elevated rocks or mossy areas above the tidal line.

WESTERN SANDPIPER (*bottom, left*)
Nome, Alaska

Ironically, this abundant shorebird inhabits grasslands, not shores. It migrates in spectacular flocks from the San Francisco Bay area to the Copper River Delta and its breeding range in western Alaska.

UPLAND SANDPIPER (*bottom, right*)
Souris River Basin NWR, North Dakota

The Upland Sandpiper, or "Upland Plover," is the "shorebird of the prairie." It nests in the grasslands of Alaska and from the Midwest to New England, often around airport fields.

STILT SANDPIPER (*left*)
Churchill, Manitoba

This sandpiper nests in rushed-meadow knolls from Alaska to Manitoba and Ontario. It can be found in fresh water ponds, bouncing its head up and down while probing its long, descended bill for mollusks.

LEAST SANDPIPER (*right*)
Churchill, Manitoba

The world's smallest shorebird, the Least Sandpiper is one of a group called "peeps." It prefers drier edges of mudflats or inland ponds. Unlike some sandpipers that flock in thousands, it groups in dozens to hundreds.

AMERICAN WOODCOCK (*top*)
Magee Marsh, Ohio

This quail-sized woodcock nests in wet, wooded areas in eastern North America. Its coloring and pattern resemble dead leaves making it difficult to see as it rocks to and fro feeling for worms beneath its feet.

WILLET (*bottom, left*)
Ding Darling NWR, Florida

The larger western species prefers wet interior locations and has a slightly different call than the lightly barred Atlantic seaboard species. Both breed farther south than other sandpipers, nesting to Baja and the Caribbean.

SNIPE (*bottom, right*)
National Bison Range, Montana

Snipe present a sporting challenge to game hunters due to their camouflaged plumage, call variations, and remote habitats. "Sniper" is a title given to shooters who prevail in bringing down an illusive mark.

RED-NECKED PHALAROPE (*opposite*)
Churchill, Manitoba

Red-necked females attract the male, establish territories, and display the breeding plumage. The bird's twirling motion in water creates a vortex upwelling prey to the surface. It is referred to as the "phalarope spin."

BLACK-BELLIED PLOVER (*top*)
Nome, Alaska

A large plover, this species roosts along the Arctic Coast. It winters from the southern Atlantic and Pacific coasts to Central America. It will feign a broken wing to divert predators away from the nest and then fly away.

AMERICAN GOLDEN-PLOVER
(*bottom, left*)
Churchill, Manitoba

The shorter-legged American Golden-Plover is very similar to the Pacific Golden-Plover. The male's white stripe extends from its face to its chest, while the Pacific's stripe extends to its tail.

PACIFIC GOLDEN-PLOVER
(*bottom, right*)
Nome, Alaska

Found in coastal flats, the Pacific Golden nests on Alaskan tundra, however, in winter it will remain on California beaches or fly to islands in the Pacific as far south as Australia.

SEMIPALMATED PLOVER (*top*)
Churchill, Manitoba

Rather than its half-webbed or semi-palmated toes, this plover is recognized by its low-high "chu-wee"; its tawny black ring under a white neck collar; and its smallish orange, black-tipped bill.

WHIMBREL (*bottom*)
Churchill, Manitoba

Coastal bird-watchers listen for the Whimbrel's "bibibibibibibi" in winter and "cur-lew" during migration. Not easily flushed from its mossy roosts, it is found in alpine spruce tundra from Alaska to central North America.

MARBLED GODWIT (*top*)
Churchill, Manitoba

When classifying the Marbled Godwit, look for its pinkish bill with black tip and long gray-brown neck or the spring-time presence of large, noisy flocks from central Alberta, through northern Minnesota.

KILLDEER (*bottom, left*)
Cuyahoga Valley National Park, Ohio

The namesake "kill-deer" call can be heard in farmlands, fields, and parking lots. In the barnyard, it appears to charge larger animals with lifted tail and feathers—like a cat might raise its back and hair.

DUNLIN (*bottom, right*)
Churchill, Manitoba

Well known across the Northern Hemisphere, the Dunlin will nest along the coastline of Alaska, on the western Hudson Bay, and in northern parts of Eurasia and then winter along coastlines to the equator.

SHORT-BILLED DOWITCHER
(*opposite*)
Churchill, Manitoba

This bird is found from southern Alaska and British Columbia to the Oregon and Virginia coastlines. With its "tu-tu, tu-tu" call, it bobs its bill in search of horseshoe or king crab roe.

AMERICAN AVOCET (*top, left*)
South Dakota

The Avocet has refined features: lithe, blue-gray legs, slender white body, black wings, lean taupe neck, teardrop face, and gracefully upturned bill. As if choreographed, mating birds circle and extend their bills skyward.

LESSER YELLOWLEGS (*bottom, left*)
Churchill, Manitoba

The Lesser Yellowlegs has brightly-colored legs that give it its name. It is often seen chasing insects and small fish through shallow water. It nests from Alaska to Quebec then winters in California and the Southeast.

BLACK-NECKED STILT (*right*)
Orange County, California

Elegantly tall, this bird has long deep-pink legs and nests near water and alkali flats in Oregon, eastern California, and the Colorado River. To cool summer nests, it "belly-soaks," using its feathers to carry water to the nest.

AMERICAN OYSTERCATCHER (*top*)
Honeymoon Island, Florida

Oystercatchers shy away from other shorebirds while nesting or feeding along northeastern and mid-Atlantic beaches, oyster bars, or salt marshes where they pry open bivalve mollusks.

LONG-BILLED CURLEW (*bottom*)
Desoto, Florida

These large shorebirds feature downward-curving bills that can be over eight inches long—aiding them in unearthing insects in Great Plains' grasslands or catching prawn along Mexican tidal mudflats.

SHORE BIRDS   159

INDEX

Credits:

Cornell Lab of Ornithology, *All About Birds*. Bird Guide. 2003. 2007. www.birds.cornell.edu/AllAboutBirds/BirdGuide.

National Audubon Society, Inc. State of the Birds USA 2004. *Audubon Magazine*. September-October 2004. 2007. http://audubon2.org/webapp/watchlist.

New Hampshire Public Television. Nature Works. *Nature Files - Animals*. 2007. http://www.nhptv.org/natureworks/nw4.htm.

Seattle Audubon Society. Bird Web. *Browse Birds*. 2005–2006. http://birdweb.org/birdweb/browse_birds.aspx.

U.S. Geological Survey. Patuxent Wildlife Research Center. *Patuxent Bird Identification InfoCenter*. Dec. 2000. 2007. www.mbrpwrc.usgs.gov/id/framlst/infocenter.html.

Waite, Mitchell. *WhatBird: The Ultimate Bird Guide*. National Geographic. 2002–2006. 2007. http://identify.whatbird.com

Note: "CC" indicates photographs that have been taken under controled conditions.